OwlCat
Faces Big Bad the Bully

Story by
Avelea Nixon
Illustrations by
Jaimi Nixon
Creative Director
Steve Nixon

© 2025 Avelea Broadhurst. All rights reserved.

No part of this book may be reproduced, stored in a retrieval system, or transmitted: by any means without the written permission of the author.

www.owlcat.ca

To Roy:

The best father a daughter could have.

It was a pleasant Sunday afternoon in the village of Catskill. All the local kitties were playing games in the amusement park.

Suddenly the fun stopped and all chaos broke loose.
Big Bad the bully and his followers came out of the forest. They were just looking for trouble.

OwlCat and his sister Sharma watched as all the local cats ran for the hills. The mean dogs laughed as they took over the park.

OwlCat and his sister Sharma watched as all the local cats ran for the hills. The mean dogs laughed as they took over the park.

OwlCat and Sharma knew that Hoo Owl would know what to do. Hoo sent OwlCat and Sharma to the deepest part of the forest to meet the wise and powerful Zandar Owl.

When they met he waved his magic feathers over both their heads and something amazing happened.

OwlCat grew strong wings and Sharma was given the loudest cat meow that any cat could possibly have.

Sharma then jumped up on OwlCat's back and with great speed they flew back towards the park. OwlCat and Sharma swooped down over the cowardly dogs and Sharma's loud meow frightened them all away.

The dogs could not stand Sharma's powerful meow.

The little dogs and Big Bad soon ran far into the Catskill Mountains and all the cats cheered.

Eventually the little dogs realized that Big Bad was nothing but a trouble maker. They went back and apologized to the cats for being so mean to them.

The cats had a meeting and decided that forgiving the dogs was the right thing to do. They invited the dogs to come into their park to play.

The End